AF268937

LET GO WITH THE LIGHTS ON

by Lexi Pelle

Write Bloody Publishing

writebloody.com

Copyright © Lexi Pelle, 2024.

All rights reserved. No part of this book may be used, performed, or reproduced in any manner whatsoever without written permission from the publisher except in the case of brief quotations embodied in critical articles or reviews.

First edition.
ISBN: 978-1949342505

Cover Design by Derrick C. Brown
Interior Layout by Nikki Steele
Edited by Jeremy Radin
Proofread by Sam Rose Preminger
Author Photo by Lexi Pelle

Type set in Bergamo.

Printed in the USA

Write Bloody Publishing
Los Angeles, CA

Support Independent Presses
writebloody.com

For my mother

"Now I am quietly waiting for
the catastrophe of my personality
to seem beautiful again,
and interesting, and modern."
-Frank O'Hara

LET GO WITH THE LIGHTS ON

"People go through life eating lamb chops and breaking their mother's
hearts."
—Eve Babitz

I.

THE SKORT

When my mother said no miniskirts
you were the compromise: deep dark
blue embroidered with flowers I had
to wait till spring to wear. I wanted
the pink tulle skirt in the window
at the Sears winter clearance sale,
to crisscross applesauce, pretzel
on the story-time mat. Why
couldn't I? Flash of bright blonde
baby hair on my legs; younger
sister, you cleaved bell, child's plate
with starch and vegetable dividers—
what is your collective noun?
A communion. Hesitation.
A misdemeanor? When a schoolboy
goes to lift you, there you'll be.

I TRY ON THE STRAPLESS TOP

while my mother is at the store, probably
squeezing lemons or searching
in her oversized pocketbook for coupons.
It's polyester, pop-star purple, and in it
I feel radiant, like the shine that coats Cassie's
learner's permit. All week it hung
in my mother's closet, dangled from the
hanger's trouser clips. God knows
where she planned on wearing it. I stand
in front of the full-length mirror that hangs
on the back of the closet door and marvel
at what my new breasts can do, can stop
from falling. The plush, perfect physics
of elastic and connective tissue. Two buoys
marking how far out into adulthood I can swim
before some lifeguard calls me back. Bandeau.
Tube top. Tunnel to privacy which I was
surprised to learn did not mean becoming
my mother. The dance of adjustment, lifting
the fabric back up after every breath—
the idea that someone somewhere could look
at a picture of me from the shoulders up
and think I was naked and be wrong about me.

THE WAY WE DRESSED IN WINTER

Infinity scarf tossed over spaghetti straps,
stockings pulled up under miniskirts.

In the snowy courtyard before school
each morning, we waved each other over

with Red Hot Rio and I Just Can't Cope
-Acabana manicures. What kept us warm

was something akin to self-expression
sliding into back seats, bouncing away

the chill in cheap boots. The boys
in their thick beanies and sloppy layers

stuffed under long sleeves—Michael
or Tommy or some other backwards

baseball cap—would try to wow us
with stories of bravery or stupidity

like when Jesse broke his hand on
his stepfather's four-door or when Frankie,

on a dare, french-kissed a frozen flagpole.
He really did. Lost a whole layer of tongue.

Stripped down to our desire
to be looked at, we wanted to go

under the chilly bleachers with who
we were or were going to be,

have little to take off and
just our breath to clothe the air.

2000'S EYEBROWS

Sometimes a little sperm-shaped, always
thin and deliberate as pop singers: Stefani,
Spears, Shakira. Sitting crisscross
on the closed toilet, Scarlett, whose mother
I never saw after 7 PM and who never
asked me if I was allowed to drink
Starbucks, said *eyebrows are sisters*
not twins, as we tweezed tiny tire irons
onto our faces using a magnifying mirror.
My mother suggested we follow our
natural shape, but of course we didn't listen.
We weeded the furrow, carefully crafted
caret symbols, as if readying ourselves to
agree with everything our boyfriends
said was over our heads. Years later,
lying on a sheet of crinkly paper on
a plastic bed, I watched the waxer blow
on the popsicle stick before the hot strip
ripped a scythe into my raw pink skin.
I know now they're out of fashion.
Bushy is back, as is strong and bold
and feathered. I'm not asking for
a comeback, all I'm trying to say is
I've spent years trying to grow out
the look of surprise on my face.

BLEACH AND TONE

Taylor folds tin foil into my hair while the teenager
to my left talks about her lousy ex. The platinum
blonde on my right says her husband wants to know
what the hell Jessica plans on doing with all those
Irish Step Dancing lessons. In this room we meet
each other's eyes in the mirror. Should I get a full
or a partial. Taylor doesn't ask about my fiancé
because I'm not wearing the ring. The air a Bechdel
of bleach. I'm looking at timestamps on my phone
when a 6-ft-something man walks in, brushes past
the receptionist, and kisses me full on the mouth.
Sorry, wrong blonde, he laughs, and looks to my right
for his wife. She looks into her lap. No one says
anything over the blow dryers, the construction
of a new gym across the street, jackhammers
jackhammering. Someone behind me clicks her
acrylics on a counter. *I want a full with bangs.*

THE PINK CHEETAH PRINT COAT

Pretty cool for a kid who watched
too much Disney channel

and threw so many peace signs
at Polaroids my Nana

had to give me a nickel
to stop. Amoebas with attitude

sashaying through a sea of
autotuned pink, pinky

promise pink, gum-poppin' pink.
Now muted tones like bone,

ecru, beige. I'm afraid I'm plain
as a stack of blank stationary—

I want someone to sense
I'm special, and I want

that specialness beyond
any specialness imagined:

a god you can understand
wouldn't be a god worth worshiping.

I want to pick the lock
of my childhood and find

the girl I never was
smiling; somewhere

inside her a celestial savannah
sprawls with neon creatures

so pretty it's violent
to want them

to be anything except
a pelt. I know

she doesn't exist—still
I stumble through

the tall grasses looking for
where she would've

dropped her spear.

EVE HAD A MOTHER

Cathy couldn't conceive
of a motherless Eve

so for her sixth period
creation myth sketch

she drew the original
woman like herself,

red-headed with freckles
fat as the first stars, and

Eve's mother in khakis
and a lime-green fanny pack,

who looked like her mother,
gorgeous Mrs. Grabowski.

Sister Anne was so damned
mad she tore the drawing

from Cathy's hands, screamed
she hadn't been paying attention.

Cathy was sent to the office
and never came back,

her mother pulled them both out
of our parish. What God

could deny this burgeoning
little L. Ron Hubbard

in a heather gray skirt,
Picasso of potential

beginnings? Cathy was
paying attention. She captured

her mother's blue cardigan
down to the seashell-shaped

buttons. Their Crayola garden
and plaid lawn chairs

I'd sipped lemonade on, the pink
Polly Pocket kiddie pool.

The Weber her mother manned
after Mr. Grabowski left

smoked in the corner
of the frame—closed

though I like to believe
if I opened it I'd find

a perfect rack of ribs.

DIET COKE

All I saw my mother drink
for years. In the diner, served
with a striped straw and shredded
paper beanie or sometimes
at Stop & Shop just before checkout,
its perfect plastic body pulled from
the squat fridge that sits underneath
the conveyor belt—but most often
sipped from a silver can on the porch.
She never asked for ice. Never dared
to dilute the fizzy pollution of artificial
sweeteners. The first time I tried it
I thought it tasted like a backhanded
compliment, surprisingly good,
the dark dizzying lake like a cactus
burped Splenda into my mouth.
The flavor so far from milk or juice,
like a fresh-squeezed robot, a supermodel's
saliva. My sister and I sat around her
like the students of Socrates and watched her
succumb to the only sweetness she ever allowed
herself. A true mother, listening
to the questions it spat into the air,
voice lifted at the end of every swallowed
sentence. *Let's play the quiet game?*
she suggested on long car trips
to Hershey or to one of Kate's soccer
tournaments and only then could we all hear it
whisper to her from the cup holder
as a speed bump puddled the lid
and she brought the spill to her lips.

ETYMOLOGY

One neon flamingo on the wall
of The Black Cat Cafe.

Why? Google tells me
Flamengo for flame-colored,

but they don't so much burn
as blush, brushed with the color

of what they consume. Haven't we
all worn hunger like that?

I've donned a tutu of too many
Pop-Tarts, the feather boa

of fat-free pudding strangled me
till I sprang for the real thing.

Slip on the stockings of salty stock
and desire, angora sweater

of asking him out first. We're all
a flamboyance of wants

we want not to want.
Where our mouths have been.

GOODS

Couldn't look the cashier in the eye
as I placed Diet Coke and cheap

concealer on the counter while
Heather hid another lip gloss

in her hoodie. Later, our loot
spread out on her living room

floor, she said to me, *Not wanting
to get caught isn't the same thing*

as being a good girl—my whole
life shifted a little on its fault

line: Morality, that meat-eating
plant, bloomed muscular guilt

in my gut. Once, I put my allowance
back in my mom's purse for her

to notice, and she didn't. Stopped
two bullies in front of a teacher.

I stood in the dark of my
father's front yard looking

into my lit bedroom window
trying to see if anything could be

seen from the street, but there was
no girl, uneven breasts straining

in a stained white bra, squeezing
at her skin. I kept a diary

of good things I didn't do
in case I died and people needed

a reason to keep loving me.
How could I think I was better

than everybody else?
Like the loose strands of hair I

unstuck from my lip gloss,
I wore myself poorly.

When we left that CVS,
Heather was the one smiling.

My goods tossed into a paper bag,
my pockets empty.

ODE TO DÉCOLLETAGE

Not the neckline, but the word:
its rain-on-cobblestone syllables
I collected as a kid along with fauna
and henceforth, hoping to drop it
like a coin into the fountain
of conversation; the promise
of plunge where something isn't
melting like a host in my mouth,
the *zhuzh* at the end—the word
my mother used for slapping
pillows into pillows that looked
exactly the same—all I've ever
wanted, to be fixed like that.

ODE TO APPLYING SLIGHTLY EXPIRED MASCARA

Can't be bothered to buy a new one,
so I break up the clumps with a whirl

of the wand inside the nearly empty
container, lean over the sink

to the toothpaste-speckled mirror
and repeat the ritual: blinking

hard onto coated bristles. I marvel
at the flecks gathered like fruit

flies around my eyes. Every morning
the decimal point of my mistakes

moves a little to the left and I
let it. Lately my life's felt like

the stye my friend Lisa eyelinered
over for weeks in sixth grade—

she said she'd rather die than show up
without her face. Before anyone sees

you, look at yourself. If your beauty
isn't truth, what else is there.

BETWEEN
after Cindy Sherman's Untitled Film Still #6

But who wouldn't want to look that good
in mismatched bra and panties? She's not
looking in the mirror she holds. Lying
on loose sheets, little rhetorical mouth
a little open. She's waiting for her
husband to come home and pull the heavy
roasting pan from the high shelf, for
her kind and lonely neighbor, dissatisfied
with his manuscript, to gaze longingly
out the window where, of course, she
won't see him looking. What I want
to know is how many steps between
pose and camera, between poem
and self. When did I decide to
hold the mirror, what had I seen
when I chose to face it away.

TEN O'CLOCK CURFEW

In the lot of Somerset's Concert in the Park I squatted
behind the open car door, skater skirt around my knees,
and peed. The scrunch of tires on gravel, and a smirk
disguised as a man turned on the high beams
of his truck to take a better look. It was the end
of summer, the chill had only just begun
to separate the floorboards my father finished
after my mother had left. If only it had been
a different truck—the boy Cassie and I followed
from QuickChek to the pizzeria to the park.
We thought beauty was something to forgive.
I watched him watch his girlfriend sing to
a field of families on beach towels eating fruit
out of Tupperware. It was one of the many nights
we lost something in a crowd we didn't know
was irretrievable. We wanted people to look
at us in our cut-offs and claw clips, natural hair
pushing through our parts like the promise of cleavage.
Cassie's digital camera dangled from her bag as
we waved our phone flashlights to find a bracelet
in the grass, laughing on our hands and knees.

"Who wants an eternity of cloud-
to-cloud bouncing, no afternoon
chocolate chip cookie in sight?
I'm against dying."

—Tara Skurtu

II.

PARABLE OF THE GIRLS

We stopped in the middle
of the pro-life walkathon

to get Pop's Pizza.
It's not like it's a race,

Grace said. We hadn't eaten
in hours, went to mass

before we began. Smoky
pepperoni, crisp drips

of cheese, the yeasty heat
swam around our shoulders.

Pizza Elmo sat on the shelf
beside Pizza Barbie

and so many jugs
of empty extra-virgin olive oil.

We each ordered a slice. Six girls
sitting on the side of the road

in baby pink shirts with block letters:
It's a child, not a choice!

scarfing down pizza on paper plates.
We wanted time to glide

like the Sharpie we used to
pen hearts on each other's hands.

I wanted a desire not even
Dawn could scrub from my skin.

I struggled to believe in
anything besides the power of

deciding between pigtails or
a pony alone in my bedroom.

What would look good
to the people watching

us walk across that finish line?
Who was going to stop us.

QUICKGLOW

So what if it's December? Anyone can stop
in this beach-themed shop to slow turn

in a cool metal booth and Lazy Susan
their bland sugar toward cinnamon—

I do. I want the vacations I can't afford
to spit on me, coconutty saliva tinged

with glittery toners. I want to watch
the girls in gecko-eyed glasses

crawl into neon coffins and come out
OK. Desire is tenuous as a string

bikini threatening to reveal the parts of me
I haven't bothered to shave. I can't stop

my mom from being one Diet Coke closer
to death or my cousin's husband from

reaching for the gun but I can go
to Quickglow and spring for Level Three:

the one with free lotion and the promise
of a *flawless, sunless finish*, and walk out

in my sweater, coat, and hat, no one
knowing what I've just done.

YOU LET US ROLLERSKATE IN THE CONDO

—That's what I want to write, not the night
I first heard you purging penne vodka

into the toilet, not what you said
on the phone those weeks I walked

to Krauser's alone: You were the biggest
one in the whole damn recovery facility.

I don't remember whose idea it was
to strap on the mud-caked skates;

Kate and I pushed back the coffee table,
the books scattered into birds.

The popcorn ceiling bursting into
butter-colored mornings in the park

before the divorce—different from
Dad's house with its sitting room

we weren't allowed to sit in. We rolled
across the wall-to-wall carpeting

in our minds. We stumbled. Our wheels
catching in the weave, we laughed

when you joined in, and trying to hold
our hands, pulled us down with you.

Falling became the game; it was funny
to trip each other, tug down hard on a sleeve.

We didn't cry when we hit the soft
carpet, didn't act like it hurt when it hurt.

ODE TO THE BOX OF RED LENTIL PASTA

left in the cookie aisle.
Probably swapped
for Milanos or a bag
of soft-baked Montauks.
Sometimes the voice
on the intercom stops
talking about savings,
stocking up on soups,
switches to a song.
A smartly dressed
blonde with too much
kale in her cart says
she likes your coat
from last season.
My mom stood
in the frozen section
of her future and swapped
the good accounting job,
black patent stilettos—
for me. What have I
put back in service
of sweetness? Regret
is where God isn't.
I like looking at
the blushing penne
pressed against
plastic: mute flutes,
rosy tunnels to nowhere,
telescopes enlarging
where the stars are not.

WHAT'S EASIER

At the nail salon, the women
pad around in paper sandals,

manicured Midases waving the gel
and glittered moods they picked

off the shelves. Under blue light,
my mother's hands harden into

pink petals. How happy I am
to carry over to her the new

Marie Claire and a Dixie cup
of juice, rifle through her tote for a tip.

I've always liked beauty best
in its beforeness, Britney blasting

while liquid liner spatters
the mirror—the mall and all

its glitzy potential, easier
than hope. All those almost-there

hours, minutes, seconds like the six
separate and smaller-than-

sequin dots that become
a flower on my big blue toe.

MARY

For three hours, I was Mary.
I wore the white dress, blue

cape, itchy rope belt cinched
at my waist. I cuddled the cold

plastic Jesus, bobbed him up
and down like he might

soon grow restless and need
me to ferry him over

the seam of his faux reality.
The priest was down the hall

gathering the rest of the nativity
props so I continued

to practice my performance.
I stuffed the hard boy up my dress

and screamed like I'd heard
the women giving birth on TV do.

A clean scream, loud and bright.
My throat hurt with what I hadn't known

I'd been waiting for. Barbed sound
streaking naked down the halls.

I continued because it made me
and the other kids laugh,

but when the priest returned and
called my performance *perverse*

they all turned quietly away.
Here's what really gets me:

The priest flinched when I handed
back the son of God I'd made

hot with my skin. The heat
not like a sun-slashed floor

in the afternoon, more like
a just-left toilet seat. Or a lake,

cold when you jump in, the summer
air colder when you get out.

Some truth in my touch bartered
with nothingness and seared us both.

THE NUNS CAME BY BUS

Shuffled up to the pale blue
and pink entrance, received

special wristbands to ride
all the rides for free.

It was my third day
working CHAIR-O-PLANES,

a metal jellyfish that thrust
tourists in the air when

I hit the green button.
What happens if I hit

the red button I'd asked
Mr. Gigliotti. He said

Don't hit the red button.
From my warm plastic booth

I watched the nuns move around
the park, ice cream leapt

from a kid's cone as they
approached a game.

They lined up and played
everything. This was the year

I decided not to make
my confirmation. I felt naked

in my spaghetti straps
and shorts as I checked

that each sister had
pulled down the metal bar

and clipped the chain
between the folds of her habit.

They rose like crows
and circled the morning sky,

arms raised. I touched
the red button, but didn't press it.

GIFTS I DID NOT WANT

A violet velvet robe
embroidered with

hundreds of lilting
LOLs. A self-help

book I didn't ask
for, but received

three copies.
A shoulder kiss.

A mist that stank
through the wrapping

and strangled
the rest of Christmas

with cinnamon—
I did it,

I touched
that third grader

he said as we
scraped plastic spoons

against the scraps
in our yogurt cups

at the school
for troubled teens.

That's what my father
called it. Cassie

called it the island
of misfit boys,

though we were there.
Eating Disorders,

cutters, druggies,
depressives—

he didn't fit in,
and when the staff

knocked into his
lunch tray or

stepped hard
on his sneakers,

I said nothing.
DON'T GIFT

RESPONSIBILITY
an animal shelter site says.

My mother used
to gift wrap empty

boxes and leave
them on the sill

as decoration.
Does it matter

what happened
to him? What's inside

the box didn't
bite my hand.

Still I abandoned it.

HIGHLIGHTS

The kids that came before
me already colored in

the pictures, circled
all the missing stuff

in the Spot The Difference
drawings. I'd look at

their marks and pretend I
would've made them, noticed

the missing pocket, vanished
vase in the waiting room.

I'm sick of stepping into rooms
certain something hidden

has disappeared. Standing in
the kitchen loving you and still

so unhappy. I finally have
my chance to make

my mark on this
blankness—the sun,

when did it stop being
that clean color-in-able

circle? Is that a bird
under your butter knife?

A watch where previously
only a wrist had been.

DISCO BALL

The disco ball has become domesticated
        like a lion that can lick a face without
                eating it, sidled up beside houseplants

                and framed photos of another Disneyland
        vacation. Gone the voracious nights,
strobed spots, bell bottoms ringing out in the church

of bodies. Consciousness is a planet
        of mirrors: the Gods of my childhood
                shine, reflect, refract

                when I get too close.
        Gourd which guards us against
solemnity. Atom of a dwindling audaciousness.

We electric-slid from the seventies to settle
        it here, sparkling among the white
                wire covers and throw pillows.

                It still does what it does.
        When was the last time I prayed
for the sake of praying? I'm tired

of pleas and promises decorating
        the next dimension with desperation:
                Let the lump mean nothing;

                the prettier poet not win
        another prize; his eyes,
stop them from lingering too long.

How can I be true in my devotion
        to the sliver of light shifting
                between the curtains—

                I can't feel it, though I see
ghost stars dancing up the wall.

ELDERLY COUPLE FOUND DEAD BURIED UNDER SNOW

The man on top
of the woman,

frozen like the slice
of wedding cake

my mother kept
for years in the freezer.

They'd been there
a week. They walked

a mile before giving
up and lying down

a hundred yards
from the house

they couldn't see
through the storm.

How close we are to
what we'll never reach.

I imagine her
in snow-soaked denim

like a pressed flower
beneath him,

what they said
in their final moment.

I'd let the flurries
melt into our

four-poster bed,
we'd roleplay

safety: *Not tonight
honey, I'm tired.*

*Pass the hand cream.
You get the light.*

CLEAN

The seam of my Snoopy PJs brushed between my thighs
and I flushed awake. My sister snoring in the bunk above.
Short fingers stirred playground mud into cake batter—slow
to separate the liquid maw of pleasure from curiosity,
it would be years before phosphenes bloomed
into badly dressed boys with tongue-moistened lips.
I was done when my mother walked in.
She picked up the discarded socks, capped the magic
markers, dropped them back into the soup can
painted with pink stars and glitter hearts.
When she bent over for a goodnight kiss she said,
Your fingers stink, and told me to go wash them.
I stood at the sink, my scent dissolving into soap—
how badly I began to want in front of the mirror;
what lifted my little life like a bloodhound's ears
to the promise of approaching bodies:
my mother's Carmex kiss I didn't wipe away,
the waxy stain shining on my forehead.

"because you do not eat
that which rips your heart with joy."

—Thomas Lux

III.

ODE TO THE WAY WE MOVE

in the inpatient eating disorder program.
Caroline G taps her foot to the tune of
pasta night. Sara takes four separate trips
to get a pair of scissors, two markers, a sheet
of paper and Scotch tape from the craft basket,
and Amanda, who signed herself in,
just admitted she's been doing crunches
on the bathroom floor. To the rules about running
and hugging and to the times we break
them, in group, when Viv's cousin drives
four hours from Vermont to play Uno
during visiting hours. Bicep curls in
the laundry room with bottles of bleach,
arm circles in the shower; how stopping
the secret exercise feels like bench-pressing
a sky swollen with rain. To the little blue
boombox we let sing to us before bed:
Man! I Feel Like A Woman! and the hairbrush
microphone Sunita mouths *let's go girls* into.
Our small rebellion in the common room
of the locked ward—we shimmy our sweats
into slip dresses, our bodies loud as a nightclub.
Hospital bracelets, bangles we raise above our heads.
Paige, former-patient-turned-night-nurse,
feather-boas me toward her with the stethoscope
and doesn't, for three minutes and forty-five seconds,
say anything about the liability of our heart rates.
We risk punishment for this, chug the chalky bottle
of Ensure, stay an extra week. Like the hooked
fish's last dance against a thrash of air, we
are trying to move toward freedom.
It's only wrong if anyone who isn't us sees.

THE BATS ARE HAVING NON-PENETRATIVE SEX IN A CHURCH

Like Christian kids,
hopped up on guilt

and hormones, looking
for a loophole—

the bat's penis is too big,
a scientist says

in the article, and
the tip is heart-shaped.

What god
of ridiculousness

blew into his kazoo
to make this morning

of sensational
headlines and half

-burnt toast?
There's laundry

to fold and
an appointment

to cancel. The dog
won't stop licking

what doesn't appear
to be a stain

from the blanket.
What's the difference

between making
love and making

do. What does
bat foreplay look

like? How do you
ask for touch,

but not too much.

THE EVERYBODY LOVES AN IRISH GIRL TEE

my mother wore to parent-teacher meetings,
to get the mail, over short-shorts and sweats—
the other mothers wore khakis and cardigans,
smiled straight as crudité when she reached
for the coffee she rested on the hood
of the little red Chevy and revealed
her smooth midriff. Our town had two
churches: Little Flower and Big Little Flower,
built to accommodate the Christians
that couldn't fit inside the original parish.
It only took a day to raise the funds.
To our well-to-do neighbors, my mother
was a corndog on a tray of caviar, an RV
in a sea of limousines, and I believed
her buxom beauty blocked my view of
a good clean childhood. I hated the cleavage
of shamrocks, the striptease of peeling script.
During a fight, my dad called her *tacky*.
She didn't change. She wore that shirt
for years, ate gas station snacks, watched
reality TV, bought scratch-offs on Sundays
for luck. Everyone should love me takes
courage. She divorced him. Fell in love
with leaving sticky notes on everything:
Good morning sunshine! on Kate's little
carton of milk, *Miss you* on the inside flap
of my math workbook, and our laughter spread
easy as spray cheese where the clothing line
divided our condo's plot of concrete from the next.

MISS HACK

from Hackensack—I'm not kidding—
made all the mothers worry
in her tight blouses, hoop earrings

like little halos tired of the missionary position.
Hannah D. showed up as her at Halloween
Spooky Stomp and Dina's dad said

real loud, *Is that kid a hooker?*
She taught social studies, but our Catholic
town didn't believe in maps that led

to places you could point to, get to
without praying. Every morning she came
to class done-up, high heels

sharp enough to break the ground
beneath the alphabet carpet, which is
what I think we were all afraid of.

We didn't want to see
her acrylics clicking against the answer
key. Here was a woman who could

ward off whispers, or perhaps they stuck
like flies to her aquanet. I didn't know
it then: she was my first God.

A gaudy god, desirable deity, lips red
as the apple I don't remember
a single one of us bringing her—

she didn't need our offerings,
she could go to the craft closet
where she kept baskets of

make-up brushes, colorful tubes
of lipstick, and a mirror. Touching up
her face in front of us before lunch

was a lesson on independence and reverence
our cubbies, the bathroom stalls, even
choosing our own research topics

couldn't teach us; she was showing us
to look at ourselves like everyone else
was watching. I didn't learn that then.

I tucked it in my ungrateful pocket
like lunch money for years later,
and Miss Hack went on

shoving herself into Spanx, sweeping
her striped highlights into a claw clip;
all that bottled beauty

she could have spent on a man
or pageant, pouring over us
like a new mystery as she circled

our wrong answers in red and
marked the missing on a clipboard
after calling out our names.

ODE TO MY MOTHER'S THONG

When she'd reach for the bargain bread
        or to smooth the fanned bangs Kate cut

with craft scissors playing beauty parlor,
        I'd see it: cotton Y peeking over her Levi's—

I remember being mad that she'd do this,
        be beyond me, not my mom, want to be

perceived as attractive. Pink with printed
        strawberries, cotton gusset, tiny bow—

she discoed the post-divorce dance of
        undressing in front of the Winnie-the-Pooh

stickered mirror and slingshot me into
        my life like the birds I color-penciled

onto computer paper, arching the single
        -line strokes to show

they were very far away.
        Now she's behind me in the pink

dressing room while I try one on
        for the first time, pull on my leggings,

and look at her in the 3-way mirror:
        Are you sure you can't see anything?

DADA

Google *Dadaist art*
and the first thing

you see is a man
with apes for eyes.

Makes you want to
collage over everything.

Siphon the rest
-lessness from

the story till
it shines

like a signed
urinal. Cut out

the missiles and
replace them

with megaphones
the size of men

or jars of mayo.
Paper over his penis

a plastic bear
with slow honey.

Your mom's diet pills
float to the ceiling

like birthday balloons.
I'm not trying

to simplify anything.
The platypus is

poisonous.
Pepper spray in

the junk drawer.
Glue an eye

over your Dad's
eye when he doesn't

believe you. He doesn't
need anything else.

RANSACKED

Papa worked security
for the old news station
between Seidler and 5th.

This was before he stole
Miss America's tiara
to buy booze.

They did a front page spread
on the pageant. Girls in gowns
like liquid chandeliers

in front of a faux garden
backdrop, smiling
like they had nothing

but cigarettes for breakfast.
After the shoot he snuck
into the dressing room,

tossed the silver sashes
with state names, shoved
aside the plastic bouquets

till he found the winner's
coronet. Diamonds
don't photograph

as well as the fake stuff;
the pawn shop wouldn't
give him squat so he gave

what he took to my mother.
I've seen the photo. She's
in a shabby communion dress,

on her head flames of ice
lick the blurry living room
behind her where Papa stands

with crossed arms, looking away.
It hurts to have to sparkle
so hard to be known. I've stolen

cash from my mother's purse
to buy Pop-Tarts I planned on
purging, lied about an assault

to feel seen. Tell me
the last time you ransacked
the room of someone else's sanity.

Show me what it looks like
to slip something shiny
under your coat.

I know it's selfish,
but I want to know all
your worst stories.

THE HONEYBEE STEALS FROM THE BUMBLEBEE

They caught it on camera
in Italy: One brash bug

took pollen right off
a bumblebee's back.

The world's smallest heist
was somewhat intimate,

she brushed the furry
behind of her victim

the way a lover might
scratch their partner's

skin. I've never done
this, though I learned

about the act as a kid
from a crass Christmas card

addressed to my father—
a shirtless Santa told

an angry Mrs. Claus
that his shoulder scrapes

came from a chimney;
on the inside someone

wrote *Love,* but didn't
sign it. You might waste

a whole life wondering
who to choose. Love

is a kind of larceny,
we touch to take

from someone what
we want not to need:

yellow dust of not-
time, not-no, not-yet.

PRAYER
after Cindy Sherman's Untitled Film Still #25

Like God, Girlhood is a kind of middle distance—
the fit and flare moment a girl decides
the noir of crying in public isn't worth ruining
her makeup. If you've checked his DMs,
his computer history, the backs of his pupils
for buxom brunettes writhing naked on
a screen, you've stood on this pier, ignited
by indignation. Soon Cindy will step out
of the scene and back behind the camera.
She'll paint on the print even more eyeliner—
the ceaseless need to cheat on truth with truth.

DID YOU KNOW THE VATICAN IS MADE OF PARTICLE BOARD

Something my stepfather said to see
if my mother would believe it.

She did. She's been to the Vatican.
How blessed the Basilica must be

that some tourist's enthusiastic
hand gestures never punctured

its pillars, Bernini's baroque
canopy never collapsed by an old

Catholic's fainting awe. A miracle
the mosaics still marvelous despite

centuries of storms. She was pissed
when he laughed, thought he wanted

to make her seem stupid, gullible—
I only believed you because

I love you, she said weeks later when
he repeated the story to his bandmates.

Who doesn't want the world to be
made of softer material? Who isn't

waiting for truth to transubstantiate
the hours spent scrubbing

sticky spaghetti from the pot.
Say the statue of David is

swiss cheese, wouldn't you want
to bite a sculpted thigh

until beauty felt a little less
unattainable? Stick a finger in

the wound of truth
like Caravaggio's Thomas

fishing around in Jesus's flesh,
tell me what you feel.

SHE OF THESEUS

Don't you want to believe
it—with just the pluck

of an eyebrow or the clip
of a rogue cuticle

you too could be new again?
Beauty is the self's

sneakiest assassin, slipping
in through the unlocked door

of desire, slashing tomorrow's
throat with its shiny switchblade.

I make the hair appointment,
get the fillers, say *I love you*

I love you like love is a soft
pillow held over the face.

I don't hate myself, I
hate the idea that I might

miss out on all the selves
I would have fun being.

I bleach my upper lip and
blanch my belief in God,

pierce a second hole into
my lobe and learn to love

listening to the rank bagpipes
of my mother's pit bull's

breath. Why tether yourself
to one body when you

can have a walk-in closet
of potential? Why

settle for timelessness when
you can tear each self

like a cheap dress and feel
the world is one

sequin on the ballgown
of the universe.

My infinity: try again
and try again. When I apply

mascara in the mirror
I open my mouth.

ACKNOWLEDGEMENTS

Mom, thank you for your bottomless encouragement and love. You're my person. I love you.

Tara, thank you for making these poems leavealoneable. Your guidance throughout the process of putting this book together has been invaluable.

Woogie, thank you for your boundless support. You are such a wonderful sounding board and friend.

Dad, you taught me to *never let the truth get in the way of a good story,* thank you.

Kate, you made me stronger by kicking my ass.

Michelle and Mario, I am so grateful to have you in my life. Thank you for everything you do.

Sara Davies, for encouraging me to stay inspired and keep writing. Your kindness and support throughout the years has been invaluable. Your students are lucky to have you.

Professor Laura Driver, your creative writing class inspired and shaped many of these poems. Thank you for being an amazing teacher and guide.

Ellen Bass, your kind words have carried me through many moments of doubt and insecurity.

Derrick Brown, thank you for believing in this book and me. Additional thanks for placing me in the world's best poetry salon.

Chibbi, Cullen, Hillary, Maria, Kayla, Conrad, Tyler, thank you for holding me accountable in the process of putting together this manuscript. I love you and your poems.

Jeremy Radin, thank you for pushing me to be a better poet. Additional thanks for your poems which gave me the courage to write many of the pieces in this book.

Buddy Wakefield, thanks for the scrupulous and creative feedback. This book would not have existed without your guidance.

Peter, Ted, and Luna, thank you for being my home.

My gratitude to the publications where these poems, sometimes in different versions, first appeared:

Barnstorm Journal
Mary

Beaver Magazine
2000s Eyebrows

Boats Against The Current
Disco Ball

Broadsided Press
Highlights

december
Ode To The Box Of Red Lentil Pasta

Crosswinds Poetry Journal
Miss Hack

Grande Dame Literary
Between
Clean
Prayer

Hidden Peak Press
Goods
She Of Theseus
The Pink Cheetah Print Coat

Ninth Letter
Ode To The Way We Move

One Art
Bleach and Tone
I Try On The Strapless Top
Ode To My Mother's Thong

Rattle
Diet Coke
The Bats Are Having Non-Penetrative Sex In A Church

Sucarnochee Review
Etymology

SWWIM
Did You Know The Vatican Is Made Of Particle Board

Teiresian
Dada
Elderly Couple Found Dead Buried Under Snow
You Let Us Rollerskate In The Condo

The Shore
Quickglow
The Nuns Came By Bus

Volume
Gifts I Did Not Want

Zenaida
The Way We Dressed In Winter
What's Easier

Lexi Pelle is a poet and editor living in New Jersey. She was the winner of the 2022 Jack McCarthy Book Prize, a Pushcart Prize nominee, and a finalist for the Prufer Poetry Prize and the Marvin Bell Poetry Prize. Her work has appeared in Rattle, Ninth Letter, SWWIM, Sucarnochee Review, and The Shore. Visit her at www.lexipelle.org

If You Like Lexi Pelle, Lexi Likes...

Open Your Mouth like a Bell by Mindy Nettifee
Slow Dance with Sasquatch by Jeremy Radin
Every Little Vanishing by Sheleen McElhinney
My, My, My, My, My by Tara Hardy
New Shoes on a Dead Horse by Sierra DeMulder

Write Bloody Publishing publishes and promotes great books of poetry every year.
We believe that poetry can change the world for the better. We are an independent press
dedicated to quality literature and book design, with an office
in Los Angeles, California.

We are grassroots, DIY, indie believers. Pull up a good book and join the family.
Support independent authors, artists, and presses.

Want to know more about Write Bloody books, authors, and events?
Join our mailing list at

www.writebloody.com

Write Bloody Books

After the Witch Hunt — Megan Falley

Aim for the Head: An Anthology of Zombie Poetry — Rob Sturma, Editor

Allow The Light: The Lost Poems of Jack McCarthy — Jessica Lohafer, Editor

Amulet — Jason Bayani

Any Psalm You Want — Khary Jackson

Atrophy — Jackson Burgess

Birthday Girl with Possum — Brendan Constantine

The Bones Below — Sierra DeMulder

Born in the Year of the Butterfly Knife — Derrick C. Brown

Bouquet of Red Flags — Taylor Mali

Bring Down the Chandeliers — Tara Hardy

Ceremony for the Choking Ghost — Karen Finneyfrock

A Constellation of Half-Lives — Seema Reza

Counting Descent — Clint Smith

Courage: Daring Poems for Gutsy Girls — Karen Finneyfrock,
Mindy Nettifee, & Rachel McKibbens, Editors

Cut to Bloom — Arhm Choi Wild

Dear Future Boyfriend — Cristin O'Keefe Aptowicz

Do Not Bring Him Water — Caitlin Scarano

Don't Smell the Floss — Matty Byloos

Drive Here and Devastate Me — Megan Falley

Drunks and Other Poems of Recovery — Jack McCarthy

The Elephant Engine High Dive Revival — Derrick C. Brown, Editor

Every Little Vanishing — Sheleen McElhinney

Everyone I Love Is a Stranger to Someone — Annelyse Gelman

Everything Is Everything — Cristin O'Keefe Aptowicz

Favorite Daughter — Nancy Huang

The Feather Room — Anis Mojgani

Floating, Brilliant, Gone — Franny Choi

Glitter in the Blood: A Poet's Manifesto for Better, Braver Writing — Mindy Nettifee

Gold That Frames the Mirror — Brandon Melendez

<table>
<tr><td>Open Your Mouth like a Bell — Mindy Nettifee</td></tr>
<tr><td>Ordinary Cruelty — Amber Flame</td></tr>
<tr><td>Our Poison Horse — Derrick C. Brown</td></tr>
<tr><td>Over the Anvil We Stretch — Anis Mojgani</td></tr>
<tr><td>Pansy — Andrea Gibson</td></tr>
<tr><td>Pecking Order — Nicole Homer</td></tr>
<tr><td>The Pocketknife Bible — Anis Mojgani</td></tr>
<tr><td>Pole Dancing to Gospel Hymns — Andrea Gibson</td></tr>
<tr><td>Racing Hummingbirds — Jeanann Verlee</td></tr>
<tr><td>Reasons to Leave the Slaughter — Ben Clark</td></tr>
<tr><td>Redhead and the Slaughter King — Megan Falley</td></tr>
<tr><td>Rise of the Trust Fall — Mindy Nettifee</td></tr>
<tr><td>Said the Manic to the Muse — Jeanann Verlee</td></tr>
<tr><td>Scandalabra — Derrick C. Brown</td></tr>
<tr><td>Slow Dance with Sasquatch — Jeremy Radin</td></tr>
<tr><td>The Smell of Good Mud — Lauren Zuniga</td></tr>
<tr><td>Some of the Children Were Listening — Lauren Sanderson</td></tr>
<tr><td>Songs from Under the River — Anis Mojgani</td></tr>
<tr><td>Strange Light — Derrick C. Brown</td></tr>
<tr><td>The Tigers, They Let Me — Anis Mojgani</td></tr>
<tr><td>Thin Ice Olympics — Jeffery McDaniel</td></tr>
<tr><td>38 Bar Blues — C.R. Avery</td></tr>
<tr><td>This Way to the Sugar — Hieu Minh Nguyen</td></tr>
<tr><td>Time Bomb Snooze Alarm — Bucky Sinister</td></tr>
<tr><td>Uh-Oh — Derrick C. Brown</td></tr>
<tr><td>Uncontrolled Experiments in Freedom — Brian S. Ellis</td></tr>
<tr><td>The Undisputed Greatest Writer of All Time — Beau Sia</td></tr>
<tr><td>The Way We Move Through Water — Lino Anunciacion</td></tr>
<tr><td>We Will Be Shelter — Andrea Gibson, Editor</td></tr>
<tr><td>What Learning Leaves — Taylor Mali</td></tr>
<tr><td>What the Night Demands — Miles Walser</td></tr>
<tr><td>Working Class Represent — Cristin O'Keefe Aptowicz</td></tr>
<tr><td>Workin' Mime to Five — Dick Richards</td></tr>
</table>

www.ingramcontent.com/pod-product-compliance
Lightning Source LLC
Chambersburg PA
CBHW021339060726
47591CB00006B/2102